Strength Like Yours

Poems by
Maurice McFadden

MAURICE MCFADDEN

BALBOA.
PRESS
A DIVISION OF HAY HOUSE

ISBN: 978-1-4525-6477-7 (s)
ISBN: 978-1-4525-6478-4 (e)

Balboa Press books may be ordered through booksellers or by contacting:

Balboa Press
A Division of Hay House
1663 Liberty Drive
Bloomington, IN 47403
www.balboapress.com
1-(877) 407-4847

Because of the dynamic nature of the Internet, any web addresses or links contained in this book may have changed since publication and may no longer be valid. The views expressed in this work are solely those of the author and do not necessarily reflect the views of the publisher, and the publisher hereby disclaims any responsibility for them.

The author of this book does not dispense medical advice or prescribe the use of any technique as a form of treatment for physical, emotional, or medical problems without the advice of a physician, either directly or indirectly. The intent of the author is only to offer information of a general nature to help you in your quest for emotional and spiritual well-being. In the event you use any of the information in this book for yourself, which is your constitutional right, the author and the publisher assume no responsibility for your actions.

Any people depicted in stock imagery provided by Thinkstock are models, and such images are being used for illustrative purposes only.
Certain stock imagery © Thinkstock.

Printed in the United States of America

Balboa Press rev. date: 12/14/2012

This book is dedicated to my grandparents.
R.I.P. Grandma Lannie Mae, Granddaddy Clyde and Grandma Ethel
To my Granddad Harold McFadden Sr., 96 years old
and still giving me wisdom and knowledge, thanks.

ACKNOWLEDGMENTS

To my Lord and Savior, the almighty supreme being. Thank you for your continued blessings and another dream fulfilled. Thanks to my family for always having my back, FTF Fo The Fam for life. Love you

Don't wait for other people to pigeonhole you or tell you what you are.
Take your first stab at branding yourself.
-Ariel Gore

When you walk in purpose, you collide with destiny.
-Dr. Bertice Berry

95 Plus

I've asked god to bless me with your longevity
I could never imagine you not here with me
Wisdom and knowledge come out of you
Like sweat dripping down foreheads
As a kid riding around with you in your Sanford and son truck
Excited about my visits to Winston-Salem
Our Sunday morning conversations
While you cook your dinner
Renewed your driver's license this year
And still cruising through town
En-lighted me about our ancestors
Lizzy and Sanko who make up our African and Caribbean roots
Some in our family call you Frisk
I just call you granddad
The closest thing I have to God walking on land
It's not too many that see four generations grow strong
Birthday parties every five years to keep you going on
Mama, my great grandmother
And your mother lived to be 104
Your 95 plus and striving for more

ABUSE IS NOT AN OPTION

What makes you
Tick, tick, tick, tick
What turn's the arm on your clock
Does making someone else miserable
Make you happy
The power
The rage
The threats
The apology
I'm sorry baby
It will never happen again
Been there, done that
For by the grace you are saved
It is a gift of God
That a bullet is not engraved
In your brain
God forgive me

AIDS VERSUS WARS

From nation to nation
I throw my hands up to pray
What's going on in this world today?
Sex, Aids denial we all suffer the hurt
We all know the world is in a state of alert
Governments paying more in debts
Than they do in health
Can we just sit around and watch the future die
We ignore and act like we don't hear the world cry
Does life mean so little that you just don't care
It's a worldwide epidemic
So we must stop the flare
If we can ask for help in times of wars
Why can't we ask for help to heal the sores?
And stop these wars

ALL THE TIMES

It's been a long time
     Since I've believed in anyone
And a longer time since someone has really cared for me
     The attention and all the things you do
They mean so much to me
     I'd given up on hope before I met you

I prayed for love and good fortune
     Since the day that I met you
The happiest moments are the ones
     The ones when I praise you
I was so afraid and scared to really get close to you
     But there is no more denial about my love for you

Today, tomorrow and forever
     We will always be together
My love will never end
     You promised and promised me
You would always be my friend

     This is for all of the times
     I wanted to say and I didn't
     This is for all the times
     I felt it and I didn't express it
     This is for all the times
     That you told me and I didn't reply
     But Jesus I love you

Ashamed Of My Name

How in the hell could I be ashamed of my name?
That is the question, I question I
How could my parents name me after a
White man I have nothing in common with
He was the French version of Americas Fred Astaire
An actor, dancer, singer, swinger
But what in the hell did that have to do with me
I didn't know it then, but I know it now
I was destine to be a star
I didn't want to use my name because I was so ashamed
I would have used any name except the one that was given to me
Had many nicknames from friends and family
But wondered why my grandfather always and forever called me MC
A trip to Cote D'Ivoire in 1999 changed my life forever
I watched my African brothers and sisters speak French to me
Respect me and my name as monsieur Mo
That was the day the devil didn't have a hold on me anymore
I was being taken on a roller coaster ride
So I had to make peace with my past
So it wouldn't spoil the present
So last week I threw out being ashamed
It was getting in my way
And replaced it with
Maurice Chevalier

Before It's To Late

From pyramid builders
To throw away people
No longer needed in this new prosperity
From slavery to the permanent underclass
The more things change
The more they've remained the same
We are still crawling out from our enslavement
African descendants are the number one incarcerated
No matter where you go
Whether you like it or not
They say equal opportunity the poor need not apply
It's survival of the fittest only the strong survive
We should be fully compensated for the ill's that's been done to us
Justice delayed is justice denied
Jesus taught freedom, justice and equality
But they love seeing a Blackman in poverty
As I lay me down to sleep
I pray to the lord my soul to keep
Give me the strength so I can wake
To teach my people before it's too late

BLACK PEARL

Looking back in time, through the corners of my mind
Rain or shine
Life's a nightmare
I never broke down and cried until you wasn't there
Played child ass games
Being a boy, not a man
I let the best thing I had just slip through my hands
Trials and tribulations, the terrible confrontation
I never blamed you for leaving this situation
You were my world, my girl
I should have treated you better my beautiful black pearl
I should have known, two was better than one

BRONX DREAD

Dreads grow on my head
It's funny what's going on inside my head
The Bronx raised a southern born dread
Born in one place and raised in another
I'm the Bronx till I die just like my sister and my brother
Yo, Laze??
Why they want to question I
I've been a Rasta since 1989
Just because I wasn't born in Jamaica
I've never been a Rasta faker
Rakim said, it ain't where you're from, it's where you're at
Jamaica, the Bronx or Africa
I'm still going to be black
In their eyes I'm still going to be black

CAN I TALK TO YOU

I'm celebrating life
No eye has seen
No ear has heard
No mind has conceived
What God has prepared for you and me?
Never say that we can't make it
Cause God will make a way
We have all been through some storms
But we are still alive
You're a gift from the almighty
Hatters are going to hate
They will kill, steal and try to destroy us
I let all men and women be liars
And God be true
So can I talk to you??
Behind every successful man is a good woman
So those giants that try to destroy us
Do die
I know that the God that I serve
And you serve has all powers
Have mercy on me
I use to be a player and a sinner
Can I believe in you to forgive me for my sins?
I know that without you in my heart
My life is meaningless
Nothing beats a failure but a try

I'm a word's smith
But words don't mean anything without actions
So can I talk to you??
There are some things you can't get from the pharmacy
Like a spiritual stress tab
Aspirin, Advil and Tylenol
Don't have anything on this
Your exterior on the outside is so beautiful
But I want to know what's going on inside
I look past the superficial
So when my exterior package changes
Will you start to change towards me??
Happiness will not make it last
But joy down on the inside will
So let's dig down deep and build our foundation
A foundation that is built on a solid rock
But a foundation is something that takes time
The lord is the king of glory
Hard times make you, they don't break you
Let's find our joy and rejoice upon our rock
Luke 6: 48 says
He is like a man which built a house
And digged deep and laid the foundation on a rock
And when the flood arose
The stream beat that house and could not shake it
For is was founded upon a rock
So can I talk to you???

CANDY

How sweet is the one that I call candie
You have me feening for some of that sweet, sweet caramel
See Hershey's Kisses form your lips
You got my taste buds crazy over your Miss Good bar
Knowing that I shouldn't have you
So I love you from afar
Thoughts of you touching me with those Butter Fingers
Allow me to get inside and massage your Cotton Candy
Having you asking can I have more of that Sugar Daddy
You can have what you want on my Payday
Walk's down 5th Avenue
While I caress your Almond Joy
What to get at your Kit Kat
So I can make your Starburst
Mr. Good and Plenty
So tell me when you want it
Now or Later

Choice's

Can you tell me what's going on?
Where did my life go wrong?
Had two great parents who made sure
My life stayed on the right path
At the age of sixteen I drifted from that path
Graduated from high school and had a child on the way
Left my childhood behind to be a grown man that day
Thought being grown would make everything alright
Pampers, milk and trying to take care of a child and me
And my pockets wasn't right
On my way to college
But it didn't last long
See I hadn't grown up yet
So after a year I was gone
So I made a choice that didn't make my parents proud
A college dropout, but I'm in the army now
Choices
The wrong ones don't make it right
And the right ones don't make it wrong
But you have choices

First Initial M

I promised my brother
And he promised me
That we would give our seeds
The first initials after we
The next generation to keep our family going strong
Four generations long
Marcello and Maurice brought forth
Malikah, Myles, Markell, Morgan, and Malik
To keep our promised
First initial M complete

For Once In My Life

No work in six months bill collectors are calling
My lights are cut off and my food is spoiling
My car has been reposed
My life is such a mess
See I've never been a person who has really been into church
But times have been hard so a prayer can't hurt
On one faithful night the lord came to me
To save my soul and make me believe

Many times in our lives we take things for granted
But I've found my solid rock and now my feet are planted
As I open my eye's I know I have to thank thee
For another glorious day that you let me see
Now with you by my side I will only grow strong
You give me strength and guidance to keep going on
If I praise your name I can never go wrong
I praise you for what you have taken me through in the past
I will not walk out on God again
Because I know this love will last

For once in my life
I know you set my soul free
Without you there would be no me
Through the trails and the pain
I'm not afraid to call your name
For once in my life

FREEDOM

The 4th is not a holiday for Blacks
Independence Day ment freedom for some
But as a black man, how can I embrace a holiday
Knowing that my ancestors shared not in the days of freedom
The Fourth is yours, not mine
You may rejoice, but I mourn
Home of the brave
Land of the Free
Destroy, Defeat my black family
Liberty or Death
Freedom or else
Till Freedom rings

GOD RESTORE ME

All my life I thought I could do it myself

Tried to be a loner didn't need anyone else

Three hundred and sixty degrees

Turn from sinful ways and claim a new life

There's a better way if you trust in Jesus Christ

By making the lord my first priority

See god is the architect of my wholeness

Never will I pray to God and he not respond to me

Only way to search for God is whole heartily

You can only find God when you search for him with your heart

I will find my place in God

So lord take me back

And restore me

Lord move in me

Help me to find you

GOOD SEX

I know what I want
And I think I know what you need
Good sex is the answer
Good sex is the key

Do you have any sex secrets you wish to share with me?
Good communication is the key
I linger to be playful
I linger to explore
But are the rewards rich behind the foreplay door
Can I stimulate you with a roving tongue?
From the soles of your feet to your erogenous zone

Don't be afraid to try something new
Only satisfaction nothing to ever hurt you
Please don't hold back there's nothing to fear
As moans of our enjoyment rings in our ears
We both take in so much as I touch your lips
Feel the waves of pleasure on our erotic trip
I touch you one way
One day differently the next
Helping to achieve that climax as we have good sex

HER COMFORT ZONE

I don't know why you are afraid to get close to me
But then again, I do
I know it's hard
But I don't want to be treated like those other tricks
What I do for you is real
I give you what I can
The cooking, The Laughter
Enjoying you, you enjoying me
Is that good enough for you??
Hang in there with me for the next year
I need a crazy ass woman to understand me
And I think you understand me
Let's learn each other
Is that too much to ask?
You told me things happen for a reason
I prayed for our friendship a long time ago
If it ends tomorrow, god blessed me already
Then again I don't want to take you out of your comfort zone
I just like being with you
When I tell you things, I mean it
Can you see it?
My sincerity shouldn't be suspect
But we are not used to this
It doesn't benefit me to play games with you
My player card is hung up now
That shit gets old

You give me hope, I have hope in you
But I don't want to be in your zone
But then again
I don't want to be alone
Love is just over rated, that's what you say
Now I know
You don't want to be in a relationship
Do you??????

HURTING OTHERS

Enslaved by the constant drinking
With a false sense of values
Making poor decisions in alcohol
As I stumble in judgment
Stupid, senseless arguments
That resulted in nothing but hurting others
I made my married life a troubled one
Married to a believer, when I was an unbeliever
A husband and father who lost focus of his duties
Why did my children have to suffer for their father's sin?
For many years I dealt with the consciousness of my past
Did a whole lot of soul searching
Conviction, knowing what is right and wrong
I was walking in darkness in desperate times
Him that loveth himself, loveth others
I believe that faith makes things happen
So I strive to be a good soldier of Jesus Christ
And stop hurting others

I Just What To Be

I just what to be
The best that I can be
So I can love you for eternity

Will you take my hand for the rest of your life?
Can I be your man for the rest of your life?
To death do us part that's a lot to ask for?
But God has blessed me with so much joy

From the first day I met you
I knew I could love you
But I had to love myself before anyone else
See good things happen to those that wait
So waiting for you was no mistake

Longevity with love
It's what I want in our relationship
It's not the clothes that you wear
Or how fine you are
It's your personality that makes you a star

See I just what to be with you for eternity

I Need You To Want This

I need you to want this
I need you to want it more than me
And you need me to want this more than you
The love, the passion, the trust
To end up bonding the both of us

I love the woman that you are
But even more I love the woman that you are destine to be
I want us to always be on the go
Craving excitement, love and fun
A true link made from god in heaven
You have such a respect for family life and children
So why wouldn't I want you in my life to bare our children
I need you to want this
I need you to want this just like me

I TAKE MY LIFE

Today I take my life
The expectation's I put on myself is just too much
I've made so many mistakes
So when do I make it right
I make it right, right now
I was looking for something I needed
But I never looked for it in myself
And that was respect
Trying to make everybody else happy
But I wasn't happy myself
So how should I do this?
Put my nine to my head
Or a whole bottle of pills, some liquor and lay till I'm dead
Once I'm gone cremate me, don't bury me
Throw my ashes over the cliffs in Hawaii, Jamaica and Africa and set
      me free
There will be no crying on this day
I lived my life partying I'm going out that way
Play me that old school hip hop r&b I grew up on
To my family and kids hold your head and be strong
Tell uncle CJ to sing me something good and send me on home
I take my own life today
Just remember me when I'm gone

I Worry About Mine

Hot steel entering your body
Blood filling your lungs
Didn't know you were going to die today?
What the hell just happen?
There is no shortage of unarmed
Black-men being shot to death by police officers
Miami, Chicago, LA, New York, VA
Forewarned is to be forearmed
Everyday I'm shocked
New revelations of madness and cold blooded brutality
They've committed murder for so long it's become second nature
Justice Department, Civil Rights Investigations
It's all bullshit
Conspiracy to destroy
Grand jury declines to indict
Trust you in our communities
To serve and protect
I worry for my son
My nephews
My brother
Myself
I'm the spook that sat by the door
You kill mine
I kill yours

Industry Cats Are Shady

Why are they censoring Hip Hop trying to put it in a cage?

I wage to make front page because I'm in rage

There trying to take me out

But it's not that simple

Lyrical gunshots to the shady one's temple

Let's take it back on the block

When they were blazing the real Hip Hop

Trying to change an artist style

Record companies be trippin

They treating you like hoes, because they are doing the pimpin

These industry punks aint nothing but crooks

Let's take them to the streets with mean lyrical right hooks

It's never too late to correct your mistakes

You industry snakes just take, take, and take

You manipulate with your corporate weight

Artists have royalties at stake

There is nothing to negotiate

So if they run up in your office and they click, click, click

It's because you been playing them like tricks with your business politics

INTOXICATING PAIN

Think of what my life would have been
If drinking wasn't my friend
I'd still be married
If drinking wasn't my friend
Product of my environment
Where did it begin?
That forty on the corner
That blunt in my hand
Started the destruction of this man
Russian roulette with my body organs
Cause drinking was my friend
Holy or unholy
Couldn't tell the difference when I was drinking
Praising false gods
Because that drink is my god
Locked up, almost lost my job
When drinking was my friend
Lost respect, family, relationships, trust
When drinking was my friend
The wine of violence
Brought embarrassment and shame
After a drunken spree death came to see me
It's interfering with god's purpose for me
When drinking was my friend

JEWEL

———∞∞∞———

Laying your head on my chest
As we rest, you're so affectionate
As I watch you sleep
At peace with life right now
So beautiful
The lion that you are
The 8th wonder of the world
On her 21st day
Nice to meet you
A fan of those boys like me
Fun loving
Spiritual minded
Family oriented
Outdoors adventuress
The form of your body is as
Gorgeous as the scenery
Of valleys, mountains and pecks
A jewel that's priceless
A precious treasure
I've got time for you to open up
Patient enough to wait
Promise to learn to love again
If love happens
It can only be a win, win situation
I'm like a child on Christmas day
I feel so blessed

LANNIE BANKS

Grand Ma, do you know how much we love you?
We love you more than life itself
You're the foundation
You gave our parents birth
Without you there would be no me
Clyde and Lannie
That's my family tree
But Sidney and Estelle brought birth to you
The Williams family is our roots
You taught us right from wrong
A country girl that kept her family strong
I remember the day you told me to get my own switch
The snap of that switch from the branch
Made my arms and legs twinge
This made my journey back to you even longer
Knowing what was in store for me
For not listening to you and I got my butt whipped
I was angry then, but I appreciate it now
Lord I wish you were around
To see how your family has grown so much
Through your kids, grand kids
Your great grand's will know your loving touch
Though some are doing better than others
Our love for you keeps us together
Never think that what you have taught us will go in vain
Lannie Banks
We will carry on the Davis and Williams's name.

LASTING LOVE

Love saying your name because with me it's real
Don't want to scare you off with the feelings I feel
Aquarius and Aries
Don't know what all that means
But God has blessed you in my life, that's what it seems
Met you through your daughter
She's such a beautiful soul
For six months tried to get at cha
But you had me on hold
The night I spent time with you
Makes my heart thump for more
Is there a lasting love in store?
Don't know what tomorrow holds for you and me
But I want to be in your life so I can see
No you, no me
What about us
If you know what love feels like can you show me?

LETTER TO MY KIDS

I hardly hear from you now and that's ok
No it's not ok
But I'm still going to love you each and everyday
My thoughts of being a father
Wasn't to be your friend
Sorry for never wanting to be your friend
Sorry for never wanting to play
Xbox, Play Station or finishing any game to the end
Sorry for coming home, but never staying in
And when I did come home I was drunk again
Sorry for ruining five lives and just not my own
You're my beautiful kids; I thank God for you everyday
But now you're gone
Please apologize to your mother's for me
I had blessings from two beautiful queens
But I just couldn't see
I was not prepared to be the father God wanted me to be
See I was searching for a purpose
And a cause that would give my life meaning
But what I did not realize until now was God had already provided me
    with the resource and material in my life of those special people
    around me
But I failed to see what was right in front of me
I was intent on measuring my life and worth by false standards
Kawana, Jennifer and Malik
I was selfish with the things I put you through
This letter is to apologize to you

Long Journey Home

As the gun firer's
To the start of my journey
God give me the will to finish
Rubber band legs
Tight as hell
Only black man in this crowd of 500 or more
But I'm comfortable with that
I've been doing this for ten years
I do this for those in need
I do this for my mother
It's a long journey home
But I'm going to make it
Car's passing blowing their horns
Cheers from on lookers
They make it worth the journey home
The heat is beating on my back
My dreads are feeling heavy
But I've never quit before
After 5, I'm good
10, I'm struggling
But when I see that last mile in front of me
I see home
I see that HIV patient
I see the that Breast Cancer survivor
I see that baby laying in the hospital with leukemia
I see me trying to save someone else's life

I'm trying to be just like my mother
Who always give's back
The finish is looking closer now
So I gasp and take that breath
I put my mind and legs into sprint mode
Claps and screams
You did a great job
One hour
48 minutes
I'm home now

MISSIN FRIEND

When we can be together for two years
Love each other one day and hate each other the next
Take the bad with the good
And the good with the bad
But I never regret one day of what we had
I guess all good things come to an end when you don't do your part
Can we go back to the beginning to the start?
It bothers me not to be by your side
Damn we could ride
The 2007 Bonnie and Clyde
Yeah we drank too much and the situation got out of hand
But my drinking lost me a friend
If I didn't drink and my pockets were right
Could we resume the fun and laughter of being so tight?
You gave up on me, but I'm not giving up on you

MISSIN U

As quite as kept can you remember when we met?
In the club sipping rum punch and sipping Moet
You were the sweetest thing I've ever known was our favorite song
And damn baby girl you are head strong
You're sent from heaven above or maybe Brooklyn love
As time went on you became my lady love
You're the air that I breath, never sweated me for my green
And always took care of your mans sexual needs
I know I messed up, but I'm crazy over you
And times been hard since our relationship is through
I know I took you for granted and I know you're uptight
But give me one more night
One more chance to make it right
Never knew what I had as I stroll the moonlight
This poem I write so to you I recite

So why was I chasen other ass when you are first class
I know your girlfriends told you that this love wouldn't last
Thoughts of me and you as I think on the past
Candlelight bubble baths as we splished and splashed
I never thought I could love, but it was easy with you
But can you tell me baby you don't think about me to
I hope you find someone you thought you found in me
Make you pain free, make you happy
You know I thank the lord for the time that we shared
My night time prayer is to erase this nightmare

I'm a king without a queen within this wilderness
Can you forgive me baby for all of the stress?
That's why you left
I didn't know I was blessed
But I will always love you and I wish you the best

My Brother, My Sister, My Friend

The beauty of one's self is inner and that is you
Positivity gravitates from your soul
We have a bond that some blood brothers and sisters don't even have
You live on the west coast
I live on the east
This blessing from the almighty was ment to be
I call you big sis
You call me your little brother
Two different fathers
Two different mothers
So tell me where this love comes from
When we have never met each other
When I needed someone to talk to
You're always there for me
You always conspire to inspire
The wise queen that you are
Gave me guidance and wisdom to see
Never shot down any of my dreams
Encouragement all around
For 10 years now you have been holding me down
So this is for my big sister that I love and respect
This is for someone that I have never met
This is for my sister that I never met
This is for you big sis, who I love and respect
With love from your brother
To my sister, my friend

NATURE'S SMILE

You dance through life with the force of mother nature
Like a wandering water fall
Reaching your goals by focusing on what matters most
Into a spacious free world
Reflecting the blue and white images that Whoosh
Off the mountains rocks are music to ones ear
You hunt, hike and fish in the hush of the wilderness
Your smile is as bright as the sunshine
The rays that come from you make my heart grow like a flower
Because of your smile you make life more beautiful
Laughter and beauty like flapping bird wings
Soaring on earth to bring forth world smile day
Your personality is the warmth of summertime heat
See I've seen the level of your kindness
And your smile brings out the best in us

NUMBER THREE

Crystal eyes that's as flawless as a diamond
Your mouth
Those whites
As beautiful and wide as the Grand Canyon
Your personality
Your swagger
Might be a little bit to much for one man
A business woman, entrepreneur
Never sitting still
Like a locomotive on the move
To purdy for yourself
To purdy for anyone else
Yeah I used your word
You make up words like a ghetto child
But your whiter than new fallen snow
Posing a mystical beauty that's enchanting
A beauty that is as simple as a songbirds melody
Tasting your tongue dancing along the seam of my lips
That's breath taking
And I want you
I want to be your light
That beacon that could reach into the darkness of your soul
But good guys come in last
So after being number three
I will wait for that call from you to be number one!

Rastafarian Faith

The Virginia department of corrections considers him a threat
10 years he has lived in segregation
23 hours a day in a cell that's the size of a bathroom
He's in segregation for a crime he didn't commit
But for a crime he will not commit, a crime against God
With dreads on his head and his Rastafarian faith
See that is what makes him a threat
How can a brother smile in a place so negative?
These walls could easily close in on him
But without Jah he wouldn't be able to handle it
Nazarite vow Numbers 6:5
There shall no razor come upon his head
We will never entertain the thought of cutting our hair
There is no burden enough to make me bow down
You must be willing to Get Up, Stand Up for your rights
Never surrender your spirit and mind
Just because they have your body confined
Wouldn't it be easier they ask just to cut my hair?
My very soul depends on the decisions I make
Strength comes from praising Jah
And my Rastafarian faith
You want me to cut my hair
And give up my faith
Never that
Not my Rastafarian faith

RED

Red is the color of fire and blood
Associated with energy, war, danger,
Strength, power, determination as well as passion, desire and love
See my gift of passion, desire and love
Was a blessing from my Father above
I have a princess that deserves the landscape of cardinal flowers
As she watches the cardinals fly
The system might have your physical body confined
Keep your strength in God, never surrender your spirit and mind
Violet is a beautiful color when you mix blue and red
Blue is my favorite color and you know what's yours from what you
        said
I love your rosy red cheeks when you laugh and speak
The devil is testing our relationship to make me weak
Some days I want to give up
But there's no chance
There will be a day I present you with
Twelve red rose's and ask you for a dance
I will lay rose petals down as they sparkle the beaches sand
Bended down on one knee as I ask you for your hand
I salute you always Ms. Red
Love You Always and Forever

ROCKY ROADS

These rocky roads is just a test
Can you handle the stress?
There are no games to be played
Longing you for the rest of my days
The devil loves playing games with us
But I will not let him mess up my happiness
We just started this
Don't you want it to last?
Me loving you
You loving me
Is that too much to ask
Rocky roads
Rocky roads
We'll have those everyday
Rocky roads
But if we love each other
Rocky roads go away

Saint Clair Street

Staunton, Virginia is where I call home now
It's a long way from the Bronx, New York
Birth place to Woodrow Wilson
The 28th president of the United States
In a little yellow house in historic downtown is where I lay my head
Reminds me of the village in New York City
Saturday mornings, farmers market
Fresh breads, spices, fruits and vegetables
Summertime, Shaken at the station
Local bands initiating the vibration to shake what god gave you
There's music playing at the top of the hill at Montgomery Park
Reminds me of the way we got down in the Bronx
In the Valley and Edenwald parks
Watching my nephews play football for Lee High School
And being proud of my city like I've lived here all my life
I found God again living on St. Clair Street
Gave my life new meaning
And forgot the undesirable things I was feeling
There's no place that I would rather be
Then in my little yellow house on St. Clair Street

STAND UP

There is a man out there whose life he's not proud of
Lost his wife and kids to alcohol and drugs
Never knew who he was
Never had self love
Said he believed in Jesus
But never read the bible words
Never put faith in Jesus
When life threw him curves
He lived a life of lies
Is there a heaven above?
Now it's time to take a stand
To become a better man
To walk the straight and narrow
Put your hands in God's hands
So stand up and take responsibilities
For the things you do in life
Let no one judge you
Get your life right with Christ
So stand up and take responsibilities for your life

Strength Like Yours

When Maya Angelou wrote Phenomenal Woman
She had to be talking about you Ma
I pray to the lord everyday to have strength like yours
Strength like yours can't be brought in stores
Watched you raise three kids
Work a full time job and get your college degree
I've seen you go through so many things
That I don't know if I could bare
You said believe in god and he would be there
The devil attacked your body
With Lupus, Breast Cancer and a back operation
But it never stopped you from your destination
We tell you to slow down but you never do
You might be in Albany, Vegas, South Carolina and Arkansas to
Love being a teacher and teaching your kids
We asked you to retire but you never did
Were so blessed with strength like yours
Maurice, Mark and Tamara
Were so glad that you're our mom

See strength like yours can't be brought in stores
Strength like yours can't be brought

STRUGGLE TO THE BACK

Hard times
A hard place to be right now
Politicians, middle class, poor
No difference for you or me
Which bills do I pay this week?
I need gas for work
How I'm I going to feed my kids this week
We all struggling now
Some choose to weather the storm like me
Some choose to rob, kill and steal
But I put my trust in God
And I put my struggles to the back

SUICIDE

Do you think about suicide?
I think about it all the time
It's been dark in my life and I can't see
I can't see any light at the end of the tunnel
I can't see my situation getting any better
My spirit is broken and I'm in a state of hopelessness
When I lost my wife and kids
I felt like suicide
When child support was taking three quarters of my check
I felt like suicide
When I didn't have a place to stay
Wondering where I would lay my head at night
I thought about suicide
Every time I take two steps forward
I got pushed four steps back
Did anyone see I was suffering deep down inside
Can I smile again?
Can I love again?
As I picked up the bible and started to read 2 Corinthians 7:6
God comforts the depressed
So I had to put my faith in god to handle my situation
What would I have achieved if I took my own life?
To leave my mother, my father, sister's, brother and kids
I had to take life for what it is
When it looked like the sun was not going to shine anymore
God put a rainbow in the sky
Suicide I denounce you!!!!!!!

THANK GOD (PART 1)

Thank you for breathing life into my lungs
Helping me to rise with the sun
See you spared my life
And brought me through
Another day I will see because of you
And I thank you
When I'm troubled I turn to you
With your praises you get me through
Glad to be in a place of warmth and love
Thanks for your strength and the works you've done
Your word is that life giving stream
My true believers you know what I mean
For all my blessings you have given to me
I just want to thank you for letting me see another day
And I thank you

THANK GOD (PART 2)

As I open my eyes oh Lord I'm still alive
Should I thank the almighty or should I thank my nine
I connive in this urban war zone to survive
So much pain and anger inside, I'm teary eyed
An attempt on me and daughters life line
She's only five and she's daddy's little sunshine

I guess I caused the drama in this world that I live
I shielded my daughter so she wouldn't get killed
I knew someone was watching because we should have been dead
I took two in the back and one in the leg
I know God is kind and it wasn't my time
My mother is telling me
Son it's a warning sign

I wasn't prepared in my life for this nightmare
But all praises due
Because our lives were spared
But if you live by the sword
You die by the sword
And just waking up in the morning is a reward
See just waking up in the morning is a reward
And I thank you

The Color Of Love

Love is the air
Love is like crawling through a wild fire trying to survive
What color is love?
Love could be white, black, purple or green
Love could be the color of fall leaves
Love is leaping, dancing, swaying
Feeling free
Love is the heart ache
When you don't call me
Love is the white beach sand
As we walk hand and hand
The rainbow after it rains
That sunset that falls
Love is an outdoor party
Laughter, food, drinks and music
I believe that love can be more than just one color
Love comes in an array of colors
Love can be what ever color you want it to be
See I've never been in love
But you bring a smile to my face
Knock, Knock
Who's there?
Love is at my front door and I'm scared

THE HUMAN TOUCH

Easy to forget about the little things
That makes such a huge difference in a relationship
Such as the human touch
Touching an arm while you have a conversation
It's a powerful effect
See we crave touch from the moment we're born
Hold them tight
Let your actions just show how much you love them
Hug, squeeze and kiss
Hold each other everyday
But never under estimate the power of touch

Thought's Of You

I have dreams, thoughts as I twist and turn
Lights dimmed as scented candles burn
I see your eye's reflect the full moon's glow
From outside my bedroom window
Will I ever suck those Samoan, Latin finger tips
As you heat my cheeks with your Latin lips
With you I want to be your creative lover
The one who is sensitive and caring
I wonder how you will feel when I caress your hair
You have a glow of sophistication that roams in the air
My weak heart throbs, this vision I can hardly bear
I vision you coming to the door wearing sexy underwear
Your nails are done, your hair is done
You're in sexual kitten mode that's numero uno
With your Latin Samoan baby girl physique
My thoughts are on you
Do you think about me?
My thoughts are on someone that became an immediate priority
Whether you believe it or not princess you're a star to me
Are you willing to be showered with love that burns as bright as the sun?
Don't think I'm crazy Aries woman, but I know you're the one
You can expect to the blessed with the greatest fire of devotion
I vision us walking hand and hand as we view Hawaii's beautiful oceans
Thoughts of you whether you want me to
I have nothing but thoughts of you

TRUST

How can I connect with you?
When you won't let me in
Trust is a big thing to me
Not saying you're not trust worthy
Something in my gut is telling
You are not telling me everything
You want me to trust you in your faithfulness
I have speculations
One side of me is like
Fuck it; don't put your heart through this again
The other side of me is saying
Give it a chance, see what happens
You talk about trusting your man and him not telling you everything
Can you return the same courtesy?
You can't hold on to your hurt
You have to get over it
I've been hurt
You've been hurt
Don't close me out
The song said
Share my life
Trust in me
You're all I want
You're everything I need
Don't clam up on me for what others have done to you
We all have fears when it comes to new relationships

But fear is a self-imposed prison
The only way to defeat fear is to move against it with spiritual weapons
        of faith and love
Trust again

VICTORY

Through all life's challenges

He keeps the words in my sight

But I just didn't see it

All he was telling me was, if I did my part

His part was guaranteed

See I was hard headed

But like my mother use to tell me

A hard head makes a soft ass

I was suffering with defeat on my way to
victory and I didn't even know it

What Could Have Been

What could it have been like?
To hold you in my arms at night
What could it have been like?
Walking on the beach holding hands under the moonlight
What could it have been like?
To make a commitment to be your man
To get on one knee one day and ask you for your hand
What could it have been like?
To take those trips that we talked about
The sweet taste of your lips as you touch my mouth
What could it have been like?
Loving life just loving you
Should have waited a little longer to tell you
So I could have had more time with you
Guess I'll never know what love feels like with you
But the love of our friendship will hopefully get me through
I won't lie this shit really hurts
To find someone that quenches your thirst
Knowing that they won't be there
Loving life loving you
What could it have been like?

WHAT HAPPENS NOW

How could our world be so beautiful one day?
And so dark the next
Never meant to make you feel uncomfortable
With saying those three words
I love you
See I loved you for the woman that you are
I loved you for the great mother that you are
I loved you for the incredible friendship
That was developing between us two
But we don't talk anymore
It's like we are strangers now
One month, two months, three months, four
Will we be able to rekindle what we had before?
I know I ran you away with some of the shit I said and did
Have I lost a beautiful woman and friend?
So what happens now?????

WHAT SHOULD I DO NOW

Dreams
We all have dreams
Some come true, some don't
But when they do come true, what do we do??
When there is a down fall within those true dreams
Athletics, movie stars, singers
that executive
Do you choose life or death?
Does that rising star that took you so far break you down enough?
To make you run to that liquor store
Medicate yourself with pain killers that are not prescribed to you
What happen to the values that got you where you are?
To being that rising star
Did you forget about the foundations that help you build your life up?
Never let the black man, the white man or any other man hold you down
Tighten up those
Boot straps and re-climb that mountain top all over again
Never let the frustration of this life be your end
So this is what you should do now
When people said you were going to be nothing
And you became something, by society's standards
You lost yourself
Be you again and rebuild.

WHITE OR BLACK

Black
White
Is your family hungry?
Mine is too
What has this economy been taking us through?
Racism
Do you go through what I go through?
It's 2011
We both see the same oh fate
Tornados, floods, unemployment
I worry about my family in South Carolina, Louisiana and Mississippi
Just like you do
Will racism stop you from being a humanitarian?
To help my family
Like I would help yours
I pray for all our families
Whether there white or black

WHO AM I???

I'm not perfect
Life is hard at times
As hard as crucible steel
Dark clouds torment me day and night
Trouble sleeping
When I fall asleep
It hurts to wake up in the morning
It's like earthquake after earthquake
To the foundation of this earth
Dependent on alcohol to numb my inner pain
I've reached the turning point in my drinking
Lord, can you help me?
I hate failure
Failure is obsolete and success is inevitable
The impossible, Is possible
Like me hiking the top of Crab Tree Falls
And at the top of those falls
I think about my pitfalls
No white beach sand
No sounds of an ocean shore inland
Missing the sound of the Bronx street corners
Missing the color of that big city life
Long distance runner for life
That's my sanity to give back to those charities
True charity gives without needing applause or credit
This is where I give myself
This is the life that God has laid out for me
So I get on with living it

New Beginning

I spent my entire life running from regrets and hiding my shame
Manipulated by memories
Allowing my past to control my future
Sabotaging my own success
Wandering through life without a purpose
God specializes in giving people a fresh start
The bible says
What happens for those whose guilt has been forgiving
What relief for those who have confessed their sins
And god has cleaned their record